Strong, Beautiful Girls

What Makes Us a Family?

Living in a Nontraditional Family

ABDO
Publishing Company

What Makes Us a Family?

Living in a Nontraditional Family

by Rachel Lynette

Content Consultant
Dr. Robyn J. A. Silverman
Child/Teen Development Expert and Success Coach
Powerful Words Character Development

Credits

Published by ABDO Publishing Company, 8000 West 78th Street, Edina, Minnesota 55439. Copyright © 2010 by Abdo Consulting Group, Inc. International copyrights reserved in all countries. No part of this book may be reproduced in any form without written permission from the publisher. The Essential Library™ is a trademark and logo of ABDO Publishing Company.

Printed in the United States.

Editor: Melissa Johnson
Interior Design and Production: Becky Daum
Cover Design: Becky Daum

Library of Congress Cataloging-in-Publication Data
Lynette, Rachel.
  What makes us a family? : living in a nontraditional family / by Rachel Lynette ; content consultant, Robyn J. A. Silverman.
      p. cm. — (Essential health : strong, beautiful girls)
  Includes index.
  ISBN 978-1-60453-756-7
  1. Family. I. Title.

  HQ734.L96 2010
  306.85—dc22

                                       2009004416

 Manufactured with paper containing at least 10% post-consumer waste

Contents

Meet Dr. Robyn

Dr. Robyn Silverman loves to spend time with young people. It's what she does best! As a child and adolescent development specialist, Dr. Robyn has devoted her time to helping girls just like you become all they can be. Throughout the Strong, Beautiful Girls series, you'll hear her expert advice as she offers wisdom on boyfriends, school, and everything in between.

An award-winning body image expert and the creator of the Powerful Words Character System, Dr. Robyn likes to look on the bright side of life. She knows how tough it is to be a young woman in today's world, and she's prepared with encouragement to help you embrace your beauty even when your "frenemies" tell you otherwise. Dr. Robyn struggled with her own body image while growing up, so she knows what you're going through.

Dr. Robyn has been told she has a rare talent—to help girls share their wildest dreams and biggest problems. Her compassion makes her a trusted friend to many girls, and she considers it a gift to be able to interact with the young people who she sees as the leaders of tomorrow. She even started a girls' group, the Sassy Sisterhood Girls Circle, to help young women pinpoint how media messages impact their lives and body confidence so they can get healthy and get happy.

As a speaker and a success coach, her powerful messages have reached thousands of people. Her expert advice has been featured in *Prevention* magazine, *Parents* magazine, and the *Washington Post*. She was even a guest editor for the Dove Self-Esteem Fund: Campaign for Real Beauty. But she has an online presence too, and her writing can be found through her blogs, www.DrRobynsBlog.com and www.BodyImageBlog.com, or through her Web site, www.DrRobynSilverman.com. Dr. Robyn also enjoys spending time with her family in Massachusetts.

Dr. Robyn believes that young people are assets to be developed, not problems to be fixed. She's out to help you become the best you can be. As she puts it, "I'm stepping up to the plate to highlight news stories gone wrong, girls gone right, and programs that help to support strengths instead of weaknesses. I'd be grateful if you'd join me."

Take It from Me

What comes to mind when you think of a family? Is it a mother, a father, and their children all living happily together in one house? Certainly this is the traditional family model, but chances are you know many kids whose families don't look like an old-fashioned television sitcom. The days when almost everyone fit into a cookie-cutter family are gone. Today, many families are headed by single parents. Others are working to blend families into stepfamilies. Some kids are being raised in foster or adoptive homes or by relatives who are not their parents. Still others are dealing with serious problems, such as a parent who is an alcoholic or in prison.

When a girl is younger, she might not think too much about her family. However, as she grows older and spends time in other people's homes, she may start to realize just how different her own family is. Adolescence is a time when most girls want to fit in with their peers and to feel accepted. Having a family that is different from the norm can make a girl feel like an outsider. She may wonder what her friends would think if they knew about her family. She also may feel like her friends do not understand her problems.

I remember when my own parents got divorced. My mom cried all the time. Then when my dad remarried I had trouble getting along with my new stepmother. It seemed like my father always took her side when we got into an argument, which really hurt my feelings. I used to get so angry with them both! My teenage self would have been shocked and surprised if she had known that my stepmother and I would become friends. Today I enjoy spending time with my stepmother, and I'm glad that my dad has found someone who makes him happy.

Every family is unique and every family has its own set of challenges, failures, joys, and successes. I hope the stories in this book will help you realize that you have many resources available to help you cope with challenging family situations. Even if you are having a tough time now, you can still grow up to be a happy and successful adult.

XOXO,
Rachel

1

The Adopted One

Have you ever looked at your family and wondered, "Who are these people and how could they possibly be related to me?" This can happen to anyone, but it's even more likely to happen to an adopted child. Although a girl whose adoption was open will know at least something about her birth parents and may even have spent time with them, a girl whose adoption was closed may not even know her birth parents' names.

As a girl grows toward adulthood, she may start to notice things that she didn't when she was younger. A girl who has been adopted may start to realize that her interests and talents aren't always the same as the other people in her family. Perhaps her family members love to hike and camp, but she would rather curl up on the couch with a good book. In middle school, she may discover a talent for art while the rest of her family can barely draw stick figures. These differences can make an adopted girl feel like she does not belong in her own family and also make her wonder about her birth parents.

A girl who has been adopted may start to realize that her interests and talents aren't always the same as the other people in her family.

An adopted girl might have questions about her birth family. She may be curious to know if she looks like her birth parents, or if she has brothers and sisters she doesn't know about. Most of all, she may wonder why her birth parents gave her up. A girl might choose to keep her feelings inside. Like Amber, she may think that talking about her birth parents would hurt her adoptive parents' feelings.

Amber's Story

Even though she was surrounded by her family, Amber had never felt so alone. As she looked at her brown-eyed, dark-haired family, she suddenly felt out of place. Her hair was blond and her eyes were pale blue.

It wasn't just that. Everyone in her family was fairly short. At 13, Amber already was taller than her mom and nearly as tall as her dad. She knew why she didn't look like the rest of her family. It was no secret; she had always known. Unlike her two older brothers and her many cousins, Amber was adopted.

Usually, it didn't bother her. In some ways, it made her feel special. She'd heard the story so many times. Even though her parents dearly loved her two older brothers, they had always wanted a little girl. Adopting Amber had been a dream come true for them.

Talk About It

- In what ways are you different from your family members? Have you ever felt that you didn't belong in your family? What did that feel like?

- Why do you think being adopted sometimes made Amber feel special?

As Amber looked around the Thanksgiving table, she reminded herself that she had a lot to be thankful for. Her family adored her, and no one had ever tried to make her feel different or like she didn't belong. At least, not until now. It had started innocently enough. Aunt Lauren asked about her piano lessons. Amber had been taking piano lessons for years. But no matter how hard she tried, she still butchered every piece—even the easy ones. Everyone else in her family could play beautifully.

When Amber confessed that she wasn't doing very well, Aunt Lauren murmured, "I guess musical talent just runs in the family." The thoughtless comment stung, and Amber realized that musical talent wasn't the only difference between her and the rest of her family.

Then Amber started to wonder. What was her birth mother—her "real" mother—doing right now? Was she sitting around a Thanksgiving table with people who also couldn't play the piano? Amber had wondered about her birth parents before, but she hadn't wanted to hurt her parents' feelings by asking about them.

Then Amber started to wonder. What was her birth mother—her "real" mother—doing right now?

Amber excused herself early and went up to her room. A few minutes later, there was a knock at her door. It was her mom.

"Hey, honey, is something wrong?" her mom asked. "You usually love spending time with your cousins."

Amber didn't want to tell her mother what was bothering her, but suddenly it all poured out. "I shouldn't be here. I don't even look like you! I'm too tall. I can't play the piano. I don't even know what my real mom looks like! Why did I have to be adopted anyway?"

For a split second, her mom looked hurt. Amber realized she should have said "birth mom" instead of "real mom." She started to apologize, but her mom stopped her.

Talk About It

- **Why didn't Amber want to tell her mother what she was upset about?**
- **Why did Amber feel bad about saying that she didn't know what her "real mom" looks like?**

"Amber, you know you are as much a part of this family as anyone. You've never seemed to care about this kind of thing before. What happened to make you feel this way?" her mother asked.

Amber told her mom what her aunt said. Amber said it had made her wonder about her birth mother.

"Well, that was a silly thing for your aunt to say, but I can see how it would make you curious. Do you really want to know about your birth mother?"

"I wouldn't want to do anything that would hurt you and dad," Amber hesitated. "But it might help me to understand who I am more."

"Okay," her mom said. "I'll be right back." She returned with a shoebox.

She took a picture out of the box. "This is your birth mother," she said, handing it to Amber. "Her name is Lisa." The picture was of a pretty blond girl who looked just a few years older than Amber. "It's just like we've always told you," her mother continued. "Your birth mother loves you very much. She placed you to us because she knew she couldn't take care of you. She wanted a better life for you."

She went on to explain how she and Amber's dad had met with Lisa before Amber was born. Throughout Amber's life, they had sent pictures to Lisa, along with notes about how she was doing in school and what was going on in her life. Lisa had written back. Her notes were in the box. Her e-mail address was there too.

Amber didn't know if she would read the notes, or if she would contact her birth mom. In the picture, her birth mother looked a lot like Amber, but she was a stranger. Amber realized then that her real mother was already there, sitting right beside her.

Talk About It

- How do you think Amber felt when she first saw the picture of her birth mother?

- Do you think Amber will contact her birth mother? If you were Amber, would you?

- What do you think makes someone your "real mother?"

Ask Dr. Robyn

Adolescence is a time for developing your own identity, separate from your family. At the same time, family provides a sense of security—a place where everything is familiar and you know you are loved. For Amber, discovering ways she was different from her family seemed to highlight the fact that she was adopted. It made her question whether she even belonged in her family. Luckily, Amber's adoptive mother was ready to help.

It's natural for an adopted girl to be curious about her birth family. Even though most adopted children know that their birth parents placed them for adoption because they could not care for them at that time, some adopted children still may feel abandoned or betrayed by their birth parents. A girl may even take it personally and wonder what was wrong with her to make her birth parents not want to keep her. These kinds of feelings can make a girl feel depressed and damage her self-esteem. If you have these feelings, it's important to remember the reasons your birth parents had for placing you with your forever family. They weren't "giving you up" or "giving up on you." They were giving you the full life they knew you deserved. They were showing great love and courage when they placed you for adoption.

Get Healthy

1. If you feel as though you don't belong in your own family, try to find things you have in common. You may find that you have more in common than you thought.

2. Sit down with one or both of your parents and look at your family photos together. Seeing how you fit in can help you realize you really do belong.

3. If you are wondering about your birth parents, don't be afraid to ask your parents. Adoptive parents know that it's natural for you to wonder about your birth parents.

4. Consider writing your birth mother a letter. Even if you don't mail it, it can help you express your feelings.

The Last Word from Rachel

It isn't unusual for an adopted girl to have mixed feelings about her adoption. Wondering about your birth parents is not a betrayal to your adoptive parents. In adolescence, you are developing your identity. You may be discovering new talents and interests, forming opinions about the world around you, and thinking about your future. Try to remember that even when you feel different from the other members of your family, they still love you, and they appreciate the person you are becoming.

2

Raised by Granny

Spending time with your grand-parents can be a lot of fun. Grandparents are known for spoiling their grandchildren during visits. But some grandchildren do more than visit their grandparents—they may find themselves being raised by their grand-parents because their actual parents are unable to take care of them. Visiting your grandparents is very different from liv-ing with them. A girl who is being raised by her grandparents may have to do more around the house, especially if her grandparents are in poor health. Grandparents may not be able to do some of the things that parents often do, such as coaching a sports team or going on a camping trip. In some cases, money can be a problem if the grandparents are retired or living on a fixed income. Julia loves her grandparents and is grateful that they take care of her and her little brother. But she knows it can be frustrating too.

Julia's Story

"It's your turn, Julia."

"Oh, right." Julia moved one of her checkers forward. Her grandpa responded with a triple jump.

"Mind not on the game?" her grandpa asked.

"Sorry, maybe I should just go to bed," Julia replied.

Julia went upstairs to her room, even though it wasn't even nine o'clock. Her grandpa was right; her mind wasn't on the game. It was on the school dance. It was happening at that very moment, and she wasn't there. She'd wanted to go so much! Her friends had all gone, and Jason was going to be there. Jason was so cute and everyone said that he liked her.

Grandparents may not be able to do some of the things that parents often do, such as coaching a sports team or going on a camping trip.

But her grandparents never drove after dark and the dance didn't end until eleven o'clock. Julia had tried to get a ride with one of her friends, but Nicole's car was already full, Callie lived in the other direction, and Mara was being picked up by her dad, who lived really far away and never gave anyone a ride.

Talk About It

- Have you ever not been able to go to an event that you really wanted to attend? What did it feel like?

- Can you think of another way that Julia might have been able to get to the dance?

Sometimes, Julia hated living with her grandparents. She knew that they loved her and her little brother, Aiden, and that they were doing the best they could, but it just wasn't fair! It wasn't at all like living with real parents. Her grandpa was tired a lot. He took a nap almost every day. Her grandma had really bad arthritis that made it hard for her to do the simplest things. Often, it was Julia who had to do the housework or cook dinner.

Julia knew that she should be grateful. If not for her grandma and grandpa, who knows where she and Aiden would have ended up? Her parents had both died in a car crash when she was four years old. Still, it was just really difficult to feel grateful when she was missing the dance!

Talk About It

- What are some ways that living with your grandparents might be different from living with your parents?

- Would you want to live with your grandparents? Why or why not?

- How would you feel if you were in Julia's place?

Julia slept restlessly that night. Around two in the morning, she woke up and couldn't fall back asleep. She decided to go downstairs for a snack. When she got to the kitchen, she was surprised to see a light on. Her grandma was at the table sipping a cup of tea.

"Grandma, what are you doing up so late?" she asked.

"Oh, sometimes I can't sleep, so I come down here for a cup of tea," her grandma answered. "Would you like to join me? I think there are still some cookies in the jar."

Julia put some cookies on a plate and sat down at the table. They were quiet for a few minutes. Then her grandma said, "I'm sorry about the dance. I know you really wanted to go."

"It's okay. Maybe next time," Julia said.

"You know, your grandpa and I have always done our best to take care of you and Aiden," her grandma said. "But I am beginning to wonder if we are doing a good enough job."

Julia started to say something, but her grandma stopped her. "There's something I need to tell you. I've been talking with your Aunt Sasha. She says that if you want, you could go live with her in the city. It would be a big change—you'd have to change schools. Since she works, you'd be on your own after school. But, you are 14 now, and you two have always been close."

"You know, your grandpa and I have always done our best to take care of you and Aiden," her grandma said.

"What about Aiden?" Julia asked.

"He'd stay here with us," her grandma replied.

Julia didn't know what to say. Aunt Sasha was her father's younger sister. She had still been in college when Julia's parents had died. But now she had a good job with an advertising firm and an apartment of her own. When Julia was little, Aunt Sasha came to visit her at least once a week. Now that Julia was older, she took the bus into the city to visit. Sometimes she stayed overnight on the weekends. It would be amazing to live with Aunt Sasha. But she would have to change schools. When would she see her friends? And what about Aiden? What about her grandma and grandpa?

"That would be really different, Grandma." Julia paused. "Let me think about it for a while."

"Of course, dear. Take all the time you need," her grandma replied. She squeezed her close. "Whatever you choose, remember that your grandpa and I love you very much."

Talk About It

- Do you think it was hard for Julia's grandma to consider letting her live with Aunt Sasha?

- Julia has a big decision ahead of her. What things should she consider? What do you think she should do?

Ask Dr. Robyn

Sometimes life does not go as planned. Most grandparents don't plan on raising their own grandchildren. It can be a big adjustment for everyone. A girl who is being raised by her grandparents may feel as if her family is very different from the families of her peers. It can feel strange to have your grandparents come to school events when everyone else is there with their parents. Like Julia, grandchildren may have to take on more chores at home. They may become frustrated if their grandparents cannot keep up with the physical demands of raising kids.

Often, grandparents take over because the parents cannot or will not take care of their own children. A girl in this situation may feel resentment toward her parents but miss them at the same time. It can be challenging for a girl to accept that her grandparents can actually take better care of her than her parents.

Take time to get to know your grandparents as people. Listen to their stories, ask them for their advice, and find out how they got to where they are today. A lifetime of experience gives them a unique perspective that can help you make better choices. While you may not be able to do everything you'd like to do, make adjustments and do activities that your grandparents can do with you.

Get Healthy

1. Raising kids is a lot of work, especially for an older person, but it can be fun too. Find activities you all enjoy so you can bond with your grandparents.

2. Advance planning can go a long way toward keeping everything in your family running smoothly. If you think about potential conflicts or problems in advance, such as needing a ride at night, you'll have a better chance of finding a solution that works for everyone.

3. Whatever your family situation, get to know your grandparents or other family elders. You'll learn a lot about your family's history while brightening your relative's day.

The Last Word from Rachel

In many cultures, older people are respected and revered because they have more life experience and wisdom than younger people. There may be a lot that you can learn from your grandparents. In addition, your grandparents can tell you a lot about your family heritage. Consider asking them about their own childhoods. Not only will you learn more about them, but by remembering what it was like to be teenagers, your grandparents are also more likely to understand some of the challenges you are facing.

3

Visiting Daddy

If you have done something wrong, your parents might ground you as punishment. When an adult does something wrong, the consequences are much more serious. An adult who breaks the law may be arrested and taken to jail. He or she will have to go to court and might be convicted of a crime and sent to prison.

When a parent is sent to prison, the rest of the family must adjust to that person's absence, perhaps for many years. The long absence of the person in prison can strain family bonds. It is easy for the rest of the family to grow apart from the incarcerated parent. A girl whose parent has been incarcerated may need to take on more adult responsibilities to make up for her parent's absence. She may feel embarrassed because her parent is in prison and try to hide it from her friends. She may also feel angry with her parent for breaking the law and for putting her family in such a difficult situation. Read Talia's story to find out how she handled her angry feelings.

Talia's Story

Talia and her mother did not talk much on the long drive to the state prison. Soon, Talia would see her father for the first time in nearly two years. That was when the police had come to Talia's house and taken her father away in handcuffs. He had been found guilty in court, and now he was serving five years in prison for stealing money from the company he had worked for.

Things had been hard for Talia's family since her father had been arrested. Her mother was sad a lot of the time, and money was tight.

Things had been hard for Talia's family since her father had been arrested. Her mother was sad a lot of the time, and money was tight. A few months after his arrest, they had moved from their large house into a tiny apartment. Her mom had started working a second job. Sometimes, Talia had to stay by herself until nearly midnight.

Talk About It

- How do you think Talia feels about her father being in prison? How would you feel if it were your father?

- Do you know anyone in prison? Why is he or she there?

- What do you think would be the most difficult thing about having a parent in prison?

Even though Talia had felt angry with her dad for what he had done, she still wanted to visit him. The problem was that he refused to allow her to visit. He would not even talk to Talia on the phone. But he did write letters. In his letters, Talia's father explained that he was ashamed of what he had done, and he did not want her to see him in prison. But last month, Talia had found a way to change his mind. She had turned 12 years old, and she'd only asked for one thing for her birthday: to visit her father. He had agreed to grant her birthday wish.

Talk About It

- **Do you think it was fair of Talia's father not to let her visit him? Why or why not?**

- **How would it feel not to see your father for two years?**

- **How do you think Talia will feel when she sees her father?**

Now that the day was finally here, Talia wasn't sure it was such a good idea. What would she say to him? Would it be like visiting a stranger?

When Talia and her mom got to the prison, they had to wait in a long line with other visitors. Then they were searched by prison guards to make sure they weren't bringing anything that wasn't allowed into the prison. Finally, another guard led them into the visiting room. The room was big, with lots of chairs and tables. It was easy to tell who the prisoners were because they wore orange jumpsuits. There were a lot of guards watching everything that went on. Talia's father was waiting for them.

Talia was shocked by how different he looked. He seemed smaller, but that was probably because she had grown bigger. He looked much older than she remembered—and tired too. But then he smiled at her, and he looked like the dad she remembered. Talia's father hugged her for a long time. He hugged her mother too, but then she went to sit at another table so Talia could have time alone with her dad.

It was easy to tell who the prisoners were because they wore orange jumpsuits.

Talk About It

- **How do you think Talia felt with all the guards around?**
- **What do you think it's like to live in prison?**
- **How do you think Talia's father felt when he saw her?**

For a while it was easy for Talia to talk to her dad. He asked about school and her friends. He made jokes, just like he always had. He didn't feel like a stranger at all. But then his face got serious and he said, "Talia, I know that I have said I'm sorry in my letters, but I want you to hear it from me in person. I know what I did was wrong, and I'm paying for it now . . ."

"We're all paying for it," Talia interrupted. She could feel herself getting upset. "Every day mom pays for what you did. You don't see her when she comes home from a late shift at work. You don't see how tired she is. You don't see her crying. You don't see how much she misses you, how much we both miss you!"

Talia felt the lump in her throat and the tears running down her face.

Talia's father looked down at the table. "You're right, Tal," he said quietly. "I'm so very sorry, and all I can do is hope that someday you'll forgive me."

Talk About It

- **Does Talia have a right to be angry with her father?**

- **Do you think Talia will ever forgive her father? If you were in her situation, would you?**

Ask Dr. Robyn

When a parent goes to prison, it can feel like the entire family is being punished. Suddenly, you are living in a one-parent household. It may be difficult for the parent at home to make ends meet and parent by himself or herself. In addition, you may have many conflicting feelings about the parent who is in prison. You may wonder why your parent did what he or she did, and if your parent is a bad person for breaking the law. You may feel sad and confused. You may feel angry with your parent and yet miss him or her.

Visiting your parent in jail can help. Your parent may be able to answer your questions and help you work out your feelings. However, some children do not want to visit their parent in prison. You may feel very angry with your parent. It is okay to have all these feelings, and it is okay to choose not to visit.

Writing letters to your parent can help you express your feelings and keep the lines of communication open, even if you're not ready to communicate face-to-face. Remember, there is great power in forgiveness—you might not forget what your parent has done, but when you can let the anger go, you can start to heal.

Get Healthy

1. Many girls are ashamed to have a parent in prison and want to keep it secret. You don't owe anyone an explanation, but it may help to find someone you trust to talk to. Relatives, teachers, counselors, or religious leaders are all good choices.

2. Communication is important. Try to write letters, talk on the phone, and visit if you choose. It may help to write your feelings down in a journal or diary.

3. Find a community organization that helps families going through similar experiences.

4. Stay active to keep your own life moving forward. Your parents' mistakes shouldn't stop you from enjoying your life.

The Last Word from Rachel

It can be difficult for a girl to realize that her parent has broken the law. Knowing your parent has messed up so badly can be like having the rug yanked out from under you. Parents are supposed to give you strength and stability, but an incarcerated parent can't take care of you as he or she should. The time of incarceration will be difficult for your entire family. Build your network of support, and you may find that you grow into a stronger person because of what you have endured.

4

The Drinker

Parents and teachers often worry about teenagers abusing alcohol and drugs. But young people aren't the only ones in danger of abusing these substances. Adults can become alcoholics or drug addicts too. When a person becomes addicted to drugs or alcohol, his or her entire life focuses on getting and using that substance. This can make it impossible for a parent to take adequate care of his or her children. It can also make the parent unpredictable, irritable, and unable to make good choices. A parent may say and do hurtful things when using an addictive substance. Children of alcoholics may be afraid of their parents when they are intoxicated.

Children of alcoholics often try to keep what is happening at home a secret. They may feel ashamed of or even responsible for their parents' behaviors. Emily tried to keep her mother's alcoholism a secret for a long time. Could it be time for her to make a different choice?

Emily's Story

"Emily, could you see me after class?"

"Sure, Mrs. Keaton," Emily replied. Emily knew why Mrs. Keaton wanted to see her. Her mother was supposed to have met with Mrs. Keaton yesterday afternoon to talk about Emily's grades. Emily tried hard in school, but lately her grades had been slipping, especially in Mrs. Keaton's English class. It was just so hard to concentrate. She wasn't sleeping well, and she knew she wasn't eating right either. She had so much on her mind these days. It was bad enough that a meeting had been set up, but what had made it so much worse was that Emily's mom had not shown up.

Emily had done everything she could to keep this from happening. She'd reminded her mother about the meeting before she went to school, and she'd left a reminder note on the fridge. She'd looked in all her mother's favorite hiding places for bottles. But her mother was always finding new hiding places. Maybe she'd even gone to the liquor store.

Children of alcoholics often try to keep what is happening at home a secret.

When Emily came home from school, she'd found an empty bottle and her mom passed out on the couch. She'd told herself it could have been worse. What if her mother had been drunk, but hadn't passed out? Then she would have tried to go to the meeting, and that would have been a disaster. Emily had put a blanket over her mother, done her homework, and made herself soup for dinner. She'd been in bed when she heard her father come in. He had worked late, as usual.

Talk About It

- **How do you think Emily felt when she found her mother passed out on the couch?**

- **Why would it have been a disaster if her mother had tried to go to the meeting?**

- **Should Emily say something to her father about her mother's problem?**

Now Mrs. Keaton wanted to know why Emily's mother had not shown up. Emily liked Mrs. Keaton. She was a good teacher and seemed to really care about her students. Emily didn't want to lie to her, but what else could she do?

When class was over, Emily took her time gathering up her things. Mrs. Keaton shut the classroom door. "Come have a seat, Emily," she said.

Emily sat down in the chair next to Mrs. Keaton's desk. "Emily, your mother didn't show up for our meeting. Can you tell me what happened?" Mrs. Keaton asked.

Now Mrs. Keaton wanted to know why Emily's mother had not shown up.

"She wasn't feeling well," Emily replied. "But, you don't need to talk with her, really. I'll do better. I know I can get my grade up."

"I know you can too, Emily. You are a smart girl and a capable student, but I'm worried about more than just your grades. Is everything okay at home?"

Talk About It

- **Have you ever had a teacher express concern about you? What did you do?**

- **What do you think Emily should say to Mrs. Keaton?**

Emily knew this was the part where she was supposed to lie, to say that everything was fine. But that was what she had been doing for a long time, and it hadn't worked. Things had only gotten worse. She had lied to her softball coach when she'd missed too many games because her mom had been too drunk to drive her. Maybe if he'd known the truth he wouldn't have kicked her off the team. She'd lied to her grandma about why her mother couldn't come to the phone. Now her grandma hardly ever called them. She'd lied to the neighbors when they asked about why they sometimes heard her mother shouting. The neighbors said they'd call the police if that kept happening. She'd lied to her friends to keep them from coming over. The house was always a mess, and what if her mom was drunk? She couldn't let her friends see that.

Her friends were nice enough to her in school, but they never invited her to do things with them anymore. Emily felt more alone than she ever had. And she was worried. She knew her mother had a drinking problem, but what if she was an alcoholic? Wouldn't that mean her mother needed help?

Emily looked at Mrs. Keaton. She really did look concerned. Lying wasn't working. Maybe telling the truth would.

Talk About It

- **Why do you think Emily lies to everyone about what is going on at home?**

- **Have you ever lied about something that was going on at your house?**

- **Do you think Emily should tell Mrs. Keaton the truth about her mother? What do you think might happen if she does?**

Emily was ashamed of her mother's drinking and tried to hide it from other people. But by hiding the problem, she was also preventing herself from getting the help and support she needed. Children of alcoholics often find they cannot trust or depend on their alcoholic parent. They may find themselves neglected or even abused. A girl whose parent drinks might blame herself for the problems. She may think that if she were a better student or if she helped more around the house, her parent would not drink.

Once a person is addicted to drugs or alcohol, it's very difficult to stop the addictive behavior. Most people cannot do it by themselves. If you are concerned about your parent's drinking, you can talk to him or her about how you feel. But you cannot change someone else's behavior. It is not your job to take care of your parent. It is your parent's job to take care of you. If your parent is not capable of taking good care of you, you need to find responsible adults who can help.

Get Healthy

1. It's important to have a safe place where you and your siblings can go if things are out of control at home. Never let embarrassment stop you from getting help.

2. Get support! You may be able to find support in an adult you trust. In almost every community there are groups to support people living with alcoholics.

3. Statistically, children of alcoholics and drug abusers are more likely to become substance abusers themselves. It's very important that you stay away from drugs and alcohol.

4. If you suspect your friend is in this situation, offer her your support and ask if you can help. If you think she is being abused, you should tell a school counselor or another adult you trust.

The Last Word from Rachel

When a parent is addicted to drugs or alcohol, he or she cannot parent responsibly. Oftentimes a girl will try to fill in the gap herself by taking care of her parent and handling household responsibilities. A girl may also lie about what is going on at home to her friends, teachers, and other adults. If you are dealing with an alcoholic parent, the best thing you can do is stop trying to fight a battle that you cannot win by yourself. You deserve to have adults in your life whom you can count on. If you can't count on your parents, find an adult who can help.

5

An Autistic Brother

In many families, parents try to treat their children equally and fairly. Everyone is expected to behave respectfully. No one is allowed to dominate the television. No one child has to do all of the chores. However, when there is a special-needs child in the family, this may not be possible. Often, caring for a child with special needs alters the lives of everyone in the family. It can influence how the day is structured, when and what the family eats, when the family sleeps, and where they can go when they leave the house. During adolescence, it is natural for a girl to want to make more choices on her own. However, having a special-needs sibling may make some of these choices impossible. The special-needs child may need constant supervision and special care.

A girl with a special-needs sibling may find that her own needs are not being met. She may find herself wishing that her family could be like other families. She may long for alone time with her parents. Amelia found herself in just that situation. Read her story to see how she coped with the problem.

Amelia's Story

Everyone was staring at Amelia's family. No one was talking, but the restaurant was far from quiet. Amelia's ten-year-old brother, Jake, was screaming and banging his head against the table. He'd already thrown his plate and cup on the floor, shattering them both. Amelia's parents were trying unsuccessfully to calm him down. The server was frantically apologizing and saying something about a new cook.

A girl with a special-needs sibling may find that her own needs are not being met.

Amelia could feel her face growing red. She wanted to crawl under the table or run out to the car. At least no one she knew was at the restaurant tonight. A few weeks ago, a girl from school had been there with her family. Amelia had spent the entire meal silently praying that her brother wouldn't freak out. He hadn't that night, luckily.

Talk About It

- **Why do you think Jake is behaving so badly?**
- **Have you ever felt embarrassed in a public place by something a family member has done? What did you do?**
- **Why would it be worse if Jake lost control in front of someone Amelia knew from school?**

But tonight he had freaked out. As far as Amelia could tell, it was all because of a pickle. Jake had autism. He wasn't like other kids. He didn't talk much. He didn't play with other kids or even seem to notice when they were nearby. Amelia's parents told her that his brain was different than other people's brains and that he had different needs. One of the things he needed was routine. Jake liked everything to be the same. That is why Amelia's family only went to one restaurant. They always came at a time when it wasn't too crowded and sat at the same table near the back. Jake always ate the same thing: a plain hamburger, fries, and a root beer. But this time his burger wasn't the same. For some reason, the cook had put pickle slices on his burger. So Jake flipped out.

Talk About It

- Do you know someone with autism or another special need? How is he or she different from you? How is he or she the same?

- How would it feel to have a sibling who did not talk to you or even seem to notice you?

- How would you feel if your family couldn't do certain things because of your sibling?

Somehow, Amelia's parents got Jake out to the car. Amelia stayed outside while her mom tried to calm down Jake inside the car. Amelia's dad went back inside to pay the bill and talk to the server.

Amelia's dad looked tired when he got back. "I guess there was a new cook. He made a mistake. The good news is that they aren't kicking us out like the last place did. We can come back again."

"I don't want to come back," said Amelia. "Did you see the way those people looked at us? I never want to go back there again!"

"Amelia, you know it's not Jake's fault," her dad said. "And those people, they don't know he's autistic. If they knew, they'd understand."

"Did you see the way those people looked at us? I never want to go back there again!"

"It doesn't matter. It's not like anything is going to change," said Amelia.

"I know it's hard for you. It's hard for your mom and me too," her dad said.

"I just wish we didn't have to do everything with Jake," Amelia said. "He's my brother and I love him, but other families go to the movies, they go bowling, or even to a museum. We never do any of that stuff."

Her dad looked thoughtful. Then he said, "Hey, I've got an idea. How about we drop off mom and Jake at home and then you and I go for a bike ride?"

"Really? What about mom and Jake?" Amelia asked.

"They'll be fine for an hour or so, and you're right. We don't always have to do everything with Jake."

While they were biking, Amelia and her dad didn't talk about Jake at all. He asked her about school

and her friends. Then he suggested they make a weekly biking date. Amelia was surprised at how much better she felt. Amelia loved Jake, but it was hard being his sister. Most of the time, their entire family revolved around his needs. Having even a little bit of time with her dad had made a big difference.

Talk About It

- How do you think Amelia felt when her dad suggested they go for a bike ride?

- Why do you think having one-on-one time with her dad made such a big difference for Amelia?

- What else could Amelia do to make things better?

It can be very challenging to have a brother or sister with special needs. Often, children with special needs require a great deal of extra attention. A girl with a brother or sister who has special needs might become frustrated because her family is so focused on her sibling. She may feel as if her parents do not make time for her. In addition, she may have to take on extra responsibilities. Like Amelia, she might also feel occasionally embarrassed by her sibling's behavior.

A girl with a sibling who has special needs may have to be a little assertive to get her needs met. Her parents may be so overwhelmed with caring for her sibling that they start to rely on her ability to take care of herself. But even capable and responsible girls still need their parents. Amelia's father recognized that his daughter needed some one-on-one time. However, if a girl's parents don't know how she feels, they won't realize that there is a problem. Sometimes, talking can really help!

Get Healthy

1. Remember that it's normal to sometimes feel frustrated, angry, or resentful about having a sibling with special needs. Talking to someone about your feelings or writing them in a journal are healthy ways to

express feelings. Yelling or saying mean things will come with consequences.

2. If you are feeling particularly stressed out, you may need a break. Getting out for a walk or a bike ride can lift your spirits.

3. Sometimes parents of children with special needs get locked into patterns. However, there may be room for small changes. Suggest to your parents ways that you can vary your routine.

4. Talk to your parents. Doing so can help everyone feel better. Even if they seem overwhelmed with taking care of their special-needs child, don't be afraid to tell them about your needs too.

The Last Word from Rachel

Even though it can be really challenging to have a special-needs sibling, there are some positives. Having a sibling with special needs gives you the opportunity to develop traits such as patience, empathy, compassion, and tolerance for people who are different. A large part of growing up is learning to be a kind and giving person. Someday, you may be thankful for the lessons you learned from your sibling. But for now, it is important to remember that you have needs too.

6

Dad in the Military

Most girls have parents who work at safe jobs they return home from each night. It can be different for a girl who has a parent serving in one of the armed forces. People who serve in the military can be deployed to training or overseas duty at any time, sometimes without much warning. This abrupt change affects family members who are left behind. Often a girl will have to take on more responsibilities at home. She might worry about her parent, especially if she knows her parent has been sent to a dangerous location. She might not want to worry her family further by talking about her feelings and may feel that her friends who don't have parents in the military would not understand her feelings. Lily finally talked to someone who really understood.

Lily's Story

Lily checked her e-mail again, but there was nothing there. It had been three days since her father should have checked in. He hadn't called either. Lily's dad was in the army. He'd been deployed to the Middle East three months ago. At first it had been really hard. Her mom was sad a lot of the time, and everyone seemed a little lost without their dad around. But then they had started to adjust. They all still missed him, but they were getting by. E-mails and telephone calls had really helped. Lily was able to tell her dad all about what was going on in her life and hear a

They all still missed him, but they were getting by. E-mails and telephone calls had really helped.

little about how things were going for him too. Most importantly, the e-mails let all of them know their dad was still safe.

But he was three days late, and there were no e-mails. Lily could tell that her mom was worried. She tried to hide it, just as Lily did. They had never discussed it, but Lily knew that it was important to be strong so that her twin brothers wouldn't worry.

They were only five years old. They couldn't understand why their dad was gone or why he was in danger.

Talk About It

- **Why does Lily want to be strong for her brothers?**

- **Have you ever worried about the safety of someone you love? What did you worry about most?**

- **What could Lily do to worry less?**

Lily finished her homework and then checked her e-mail one more time before bed. There were still no messages from her dad. Lily had trouble falling asleep that night. She tossed and turned, imagining what could have stopped her dad from calling. What if something had happened to her dad? The news was full of stories about bombings and other violence in that part of the world. What if her father had been hurt . . . or worse?

What if something had happened to her dad? The news was full of stories about bombings and other violence in that part of the world.

Talk About It

- How do you think Lily felt when she found out that her father was going to be deployed?

- What do you think would be the most challenging thing about having a parent deployed?

- Have you ever had to be away from one or both parents for a long time? What did you do to help make it easier?

Lily had trouble concentrating on her classes the next day. At lunch her friends were all talking about what they were going to wear to the dance on Saturday. It was only Tuesday. Saturday seemed ages away. What if she still hadn't heard from her dad by then? How could she even think about something so trivial as what to wear to a dance? It wasn't long before Lily felt like she couldn't even sit at the same table as her friends. She made an excuse about finishing some homework. Lily thought she might go to the school library, but on the way there she saw Megan sitting on a bench reading a book. Lily didn't know Megan very well. Actually, Lily didn't know Megan at all. Lily was popular and had lots of friends, while Megan was more of the quiet type. But Lily had seen Megan on the base once when she'd gone to eat lunch with her dad. That meant that one of Megan's parents must be in the army too.

Talk About It

- Why did Lily have a hard time talking with her friends? Have you ever felt like your friends would not understand your feelings about a problem you had?

- If Lily had tried to talk to her friends about her dad, do you think they would have understood?

"Hey Megan?" Lily began. "Can I talk to you?"

Megan looked up from her book. She seemed surprised and a little suspicious. "Yeah, sure," she said.

Lily sat down. "Your dad's in the army, right?"

"My mom, actually," Megan replied. "Why?"

"Well, my dad is too. He got deployed three months ago."

Megan's expression softened. "My mom was deployed last year. It was tough. But she's back now."

"Really? That's good," Lily paused. "The thing is, my dad . . . we haven't heard from him, and he was supposed to call three days ago."

"Oh, my gosh, you must be totally freaking out! That happened to us too, twice. The second time was nearly a week, and I was sure . . . but she was okay!"

"Really?"

"Yeah, your dad's probably okay too. But it's hard not to know for sure."

The girls talked until the bell rang. Lily was still worried about her dad, but it helped to know that someone else had felt the same way she did.

When Lily got home, her mom met her at the front door with a big smile. "He called!" she nearly shouted. "He's fine. Communications were just down for a few days."

Lily hugged her mom. She felt lighter, as if a giant weight had been lifted off her shoulders.

That night, after she replied to her dad's e-mail, Lily looked up Megan's e-mail address in the school directory. She wanted to talk to someone she knew would understand.

Talk About It

- Why do you think it helped Lily to talk with Megan?

- Do you think Lily and Megan will become friends? Why or why not?

Ask Dr. Robyn

When a girl has a parent in the military, she is forced to think about things that a lot of other kids her age don't have to deal with. Other kids might not think too much about fighting in other countries, but a girl who has a deployed parent likely worries that her parent is in danger. Not knowing if your parent is safe can be a heavy burden to bear. In addition, many girls feel that they must hide their feelings in order to be strong for their families. Talking to someone in a similar situation really helped Lily.

It's okay to feel stressed out—having a deployed parent is a very stressful situation. But it's also important to manage your stress so that it doesn't get out of control. Frequently feeling irritable or having difficulty concentrating in school are both signs that you may be overstressed. If you are feeling stressed out, finding someone to talk to can really help. It is also important that you get enough sleep, eat nutritious foods, and get plenty of exercise to release stress and stay healthy.

Get Healthy

1. When a parent is deployed, communication is extremely important. Communicating often will help you stay connected and will let you know that your parent is safe.

2. Stay busy! Keep your mind and body busy so that your worried thoughts don't get out of control. Keeping busy will also give you new and interesting things to tell your parent in an e-mail or on the phone.

3. If your parent has been deployed to a dangerous location, don't let what you see on the news scare you too much. Wait for accurate information from your parents.

4. There is a great deal of support for the families of people who serve in the military. Get involved in a group with other teens who are in similar circumstances.

The Last Word from Rachel

Serving in the military is a big responsibility. People in the military must sacrifice a lot to serve their country. If you have a parent in the military, it might feel like your whole family is serving, not just your parent. That can be difficult if all you want is to be a normal teenager. You may have mixed feelings about your parent being in the military. You might feel proud, scared, or angry. However you feel, try to remember that your parent is doing what he or she believes is best for your family and for the country.

7

The Foster Girl

Sometimes the government puts a child into foster care. In foster care, a new family temporarily takes care of the child until the child's own family can care for him or her again, or until the child finds new adoptive parents. A girl may find herself in foster care for many different reasons. Her parents may have been abusive or neglectful. They may have mental health issues that make it impossible for them to care for a child. Sometimes, a child is abandoned or her parents die and there are no relatives who can care for her. Whatever the reason, it is never the child's fault.

Being placed in a home with strangers can be very challenging for a foster child. She will need to adjust to a new household with new rules and routines. She may not get along with her new family. In addition, she could be moved to a new home at any time. Sometimes foster children bond with one family, only to be moved to another.

A girl in a foster home may try very hard to be on her best behavior so that her foster family will want to keep her for a long time. Being on "best behavior" can be difficult for any teen. But for someone like Hannah, who had already been through a lot of hard times, it seemed like more than she could handle.

Hannah's Story

Hannah was ten years old when she and her two younger brothers were taken away from their mother by a social worker. Their mother was addicted to drugs and was not taking care of them. Hannah had been doing the best she could. She tried to make sure her brothers got breakfast and dinner, but often there was not much food in the house. When she went to school, she worried about her brothers. They were still too young for

Hannah was ten years old when she and her two younger brothers were taken away from their mother by a social worker.

kindergarten and were home alone with their mom all day. Hannah's dad was hardly ever around, and when he was, he often hit them.

When Hannah was placed in her first foster home, she was very angry. She was angry with her mother for not taking care of her. She was angry with social services because they had separated her from her brothers. She was angry with herself because she thought it was somehow all her fault.

Hannah's new foster parents were kind to her. For the first time in her life she had nice, clean clothes and plenty to eat. Hannah tried to be good. She tried to follow the rules and do what she was told. But sometimes the anger she had inside came out in uncontrollable bursts. One time, her foster sister changed the channel in the middle of a show Hannah was watching. Hannah threw the remote control at her head as hard as she could. There was a lot of blood, and her foster sister had to go to the emergency room. A few days later, Hannah was taken away and placed in a different foster home.

When Hannah was placed in her first foster home, she was very angry.

Now Hannah was 14 years old and in her fifth foster home. Her foster parents, Nancy and Fred, had already raised five children of their own. They were kind and Hannah was trying to be good, but she could feel the anger boiling inside her. She knew that someday soon, she would explode, and then she would be sent away . . . again.

It happened one day just before dinner. Hannah was setting the table when Nancy, who was draining the pasta, asked her to stir the sauce. Something in Hannah just snapped.

"How can I stir the sauce when I'm setting the table? I can't do two things at once!" she screamed and slammed a plate down on the table. The plate shattered. Hannah knew it was wrong and stupid, but seeing that plate shatter somehow made her feel a little better. She threw a second plate on the floor, then a third, then the glasses, the water pitcher, and anything else within reach, all while screaming about setting the table and stirring sauce. When there was nothing left to break, Hannah stormed off to her room.

"Stupid, stupid, stupid!" she muttered to herself as she packed her bags. She'd done it again. Why couldn't she stay in control of her temper? What was wrong with her? Now she'd have to go to a new foster home and start all over again.

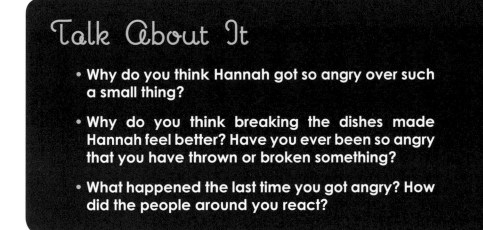

Talk About It

- Why do you think Hannah got so angry over such a small thing?

- Why do you think breaking the dishes made Hannah feel better? Have you ever been so angry that you have thrown or broken something?

- What happened the last time you got angry? How did the people around you react?

Hannah was nearly done when there was a knock on her door. When Nancy saw her packed bags, she looked genuinely puzzled.

"Hannah, don't you want to stay with us anymore?" she asked.

Hannah found she could not look Nancy in the eye. "Yeah, of course . . . you've been really nice, but . . . well, you know." Hannah motioned toward the kitchen.

"Oh, so you think we're sending you away?" asked Nancy.

"I've been sent away for less," Hannah replied.

"Well, that was quite a . . . display," said Nancy. "But I can understand why you are angry."

"Because you asked me to stir the sauce?" asked Hannah.

"I don't think that is what you were angry about. Fred and I know things haven't been easy for you. Maybe someday you can tell us about it. But for now, how about you unpack those bags and then come help me clean up the mess in the kitchen?"

Talk About It

- **What does Nancy think Hannah is really angry about? Have you ever been angry about something, but taken it out on someone else?**

- **How do you think Hannah felt when she realized that Nancy and Fred were not going to send her away?**

- **Do you think Hannah should try to talk to Nancy about her feelings?**

Ask Dr. Robyn

A girl in foster care may feel like she has very little control over her own life. She is usually given no choice about being removed from her home and biological parents. She often has very little choice about what kind of a foster home she is placed in and who will take care of her. This can be especially difficult for teens who are trying to establish a sense of independence as they grow toward adulthood. Hannah was lucky to have found a home with Nancy and Fred, but she had many challenges ahead of her. Hannah needed to learn to trust the adults in her life. This is often hard for foster children who have been disappointed with their own parents. However, learning to trust is an important part of growing up.

Often, foster children have difficulty bonding with their foster parents because they have feelings of loyalty toward their biological parents. A girl may feel that by loving her foster parents she is somehow being disloyal to her biological parents. It can help to realize that bonding with your foster parents does not need to diminish the love you feel for your biological parents. In fact, it is good to have many adults who care about you and want to help you. It can be good to know that you can go to one adult when you need help with homework and to another when you need to talk about a problem you are having with friends at school.

Get Healthy

1. Try not to push away the adults in your life. It can be tough to trust adults when they have let you down in the past, but most of the adults around you want to help.

2. Find appropriate ways to express your feelings. Don't bottle up your feelings until you explode.

3. If you make a mistake, even a big one, own up to it and apologize. Do your best to make things right and learn from your mistake so that it doesn't happen again.

4. Remember that attitude matters. Your life may be hard right now, but try to find the things that are good and focus on those.

The Last Word from Rachel

Although foster children have many challenges, there are also many happy endings. You will find adults who you can trust and depend on. Many foster children go through a lot of foster homes and group homes before they find a forever family. Even foster children who never find a family that they can really bond with can grow up to have happy and successful lives. However, growing into a responsible, well-adjusted adult requires good role models and a lot of adult support. Who is a positive role model in your life? What can you learn from that person?

8

Black and White

Many people identify strongly with their heritage. They may take pride in being Swedish, Latino, or Native American. But what about children who have parents from two different ethnicities? Ideally, a girl of mixed race will feel connected to both sides of her family. She will feel welcomed and loved by all of her relatives and feel that she can claim both heritages. However, sometimes a girl of mixed ethnicity only identifies with one side of her family, or feels that she does not belong to either group. In other cases, a girl of mixed ethnicity may feel fine about her own identity, but other people may make her feel uncomfortable about how she looks and who she is. Olivia had always felt closer to her father's side of the family. Read her story to see what happens when she starts to explore her mother's side.

Olivia's Story

Olivia's father was black and her mother was white. Olivia's skin was lighter than her father's but not nearly as light as her mother's. Most people who saw her thought she was black. Sometimes, people who didn't know them seemed a little surprised when they saw Olivia and her mother together in public. Some people even asked if she was adopted. Olivia thought it was rude for a stranger to ask such a personal question, but her mother had more

Sometimes, people who didn't know them seemed a little surprised when they saw Olivia and her mother together in public.

patience. Her mother would explain that her husband was black and add something about how lucky they were to have such a beautiful child.

Even though Olivia was an only child, her family never felt small. Olivia and her parents spent a lot of time with her father's relatives. Grandma Sophie and Grandpa Jim had a big house just down the street, and they always had Sunday dinner there, along with all of Olivia's aunts, uncles, and cousins. It was a

little chaotic, but Olivia didn't mind. She loved the big family dinners. Olivia would often stop by her grandparents' house on her way home from school.

Her grandma always had a plate of cookies waiting for her. Sometimes they played a board game or worked on a jigsaw puzzle. Other times, Olivia's grandma told her stories about when she was a girl.

Olivia didn't know her other grandmother nearly as well. She only saw her once a year when she and her mother flew to Indiana. Her dad never came with them. They would stay with Grandma Eliza for a few uncomfortable days and then fly home. Olivia had always been afraid of Grandma Eliza. She never talked much to Olivia, and when she did it was usually to criticize her. Olivia was nervous because the trip was coming up in just a few weeks.

Olivia didn't know her other grandmother nearly as well. She only saw her once a year when she and her mother flew to Indiana.

Talk About It

- **Why do you think Olivia only sees Grandma Eliza once a year?**

- **Why do you think Olivia's father never goes to Indiana with Olivia and her mother?**

One day during the visit, Olivia was reading in the living room when Grandma Eliza walked in. She asked Olivia what she was reading, so Olivia showed her the book.

"What's your book about?" her grandma asked.

"It's about a girl who falls in love with a werewolf," said Olivia.

"Why would a girl want to do a thing like that? It sounds dangerous and stupid."

Olivia thought a moment before answering. "Well, it is dangerous. The werewolf is always tempted to kill her, but he never does because he loves her."

"Love isn't everything, you know," said her grandma. "The girl would be better off if she stuck to her own kind."

Olivia suddenly felt brave. "Is that what you think about my mom? Would you have been happier if she'd stuck to her own kind and married someone white instead of my dad?"

Grandma Eliza looked surprised by her question. "Is that what your mother told you?"

"No, but I'm not stupid. I hear things. I see things. Have you even met my dad?"

"No. I have never met your father and I never plan to. I don't expect you to understand, but your mother knows she went against my wishes when she married that man."

Talk About It

- **Why do you think Grandma Eliza did not want her daughter to marry Olivia's father?**

- **How do you think Olivia's mother felt when her mother refused to meet her husband?**

- **How do you think hearing what her grandma thinks of her father makes Olivia feel?**

"But Grandma, they love each other. Mom and Dad are happy together. And, well, there's me. Do you think that I never should have been born?" Olivia asked.

Grandma Eliza looked at Olivia for a long moment and didn't say anything. Olivia felt like she was about to cry. Did her own grandma wish she had never been born?

Olivia refused to let Grandma Eliza see her cry. She got up to leave the room, but just as she got to the door, she heard her grandma's voice.

"Wait," her grandma said. Olivia stopped. "No. Of course I don't wish you'd never been born. I'm so sorry, Olivia. Please come back and let's talk about it."

Talk About It

- Do you think Olivia's grandma is telling the truth? Why or why not?

- What do you think Olivia's grandma will say to explain how she feels about her daughter's marriage?

- Do you think people can change their beliefs? Is it possible for Grandma Eliza to change how she feels about Olivia's father?

Olivia felt at home with her black relatives because she spent a lot of time with them. In addition, because her skin was dark and her features resembled those on her father's side, she probably felt like she fit in with them. She might have felt equally at home with her grandma Eliza if she had spent more time with her and if her grandma had not been negative about her parents' marriage. It could be that Olivia's grandma is ready to rethink her own beliefs about race.

You can't control the beliefs that other people have, but you can control how you feel about yourself. You can feel proud of yourself, proud of your accomplishments, and proud of your cultural background. Children of mixed ethnicity are a part of at least two different heritages, each of which has its own customs and traditions. By learning about your heritage and all the things that make up who you are, you learn about yourself.

Get Healthy

1. Learn about your heritage. Find out if there are groups or community celebrations in which you and your family can participate.

2. When people ask you blunt or inappropriate questions about your heritage, try to be

patient and polite. By answering their questions, you can help promote understanding and tolerance.

3. If you feel that you don't relate well to one side of your family, try to find ways to connect with them. What do you have in common with the people on that side of the family? How are you the same?

4. Remember, color is only skin deep. Don't make assumptions about people based on their appearance.

The Last Word from Rachel

Years ago, interracial marriage was discouraged by most people and was even illegal in some places in the United States. Fortunately, opinions and laws have changed, and today it is more and more common to see mixed marriages. If you are of mixed ethnicity, you are not alone. Remember to embrace this unique and beautiful part of yourself. Perhaps someday there will be more mixed-ethnicity people than people who are not of mixed ethnicity. Even though there are more people of mixed ethnicity than ever before, some people still stare or make insensitive comments. If this ever happens to you, remember that it says more about the ignorance or intolerance of the person making the comments than it does about you.

9

Mom and Mom

Most families start with a mom and a dad, but what about gay and lesbian couples who have children? Although children of same-sex parents may sometimes feel like they are missing out on having a parent of both genders, most say that they don't mind being raised by two moms or two dads. However, they do say that teasing and bullying from other kids is a big problem. A girl who has same-sex parents may find that she is the center of unwelcome attention at school.

Although people have become much more toler-
ant and accepting of same-sex couples in recent years,
many people still behave disrespectfully toward gay
people. While many gay and lesbian teens are "coming out," others are still not ready to take that step.
Straight children of gay parents may face some of the
same challenges. They may not want their peers to
know that their parents are lesbian or gay. What wasn't
a big deal in first or second grade can become a bigger
challenge by middle school as kids become more aware
of sex and what it means to be gay or straight. Read
Taylor's story to see what happened to her when her
classmates found out about her two moms.

Taylor's Story

Everything changed for Taylor the day after her first
school basketball game. Both of her mothers had come
to see her play. She'd done well and even made a few
baskets, but in the end, that wasn't what mattered.

Taylor knew something was wrong almost as
soon as she got off the bus.
Kids were looking at her,
whispering and pointing.
Her friends were nowhere
in sight. When she saw her
locker, she stopped in her
tracks. On her locker, the word LESBIAN was scrawled
in big, black letters. Kids were standing around looking and laughing.

A girl who has same-sex parents may find that she is the center of unwelcome attention at school.

By lunchtime, her locker had been cleaned and the kids who did it had been suspended, but nothing was the same as it had been. Every day after that, kids called her names in the halls. Sometimes she was even shoved from behind or tripped in the hall. She had made a lot of new friends at the start of the school year, but now most of them were ignoring her. Basketball wasn't fun anymore. Most of the time, the other girls wouldn't even pass the ball to her.

Talk About It

- **How do you think Taylor felt when she saw her locker?**

- **Have you ever had kids say or write anything bad about you? Was it true? How did it make you feel?**

- **Is there anything Taylor can do to make things better at school?**

Usually, Taylor didn't mind having two moms. They were both great. They both loved her and she'd never really missed having a dad. Taylor was pretty sure she was not a lesbian herself. She liked boys. It was stupid for others to think that just because she was raised by lesbians she was one too. But she knew there was no point trying to tell that to the kids at school.

Taylor didn't tell her moms what was happening. They knew about the locker incident because the principal had called them. Taylor had tried to make it sound like it was no big deal. In the past, it hadn't been. She'd been teased before, but not very much. Most of the kids in her elementary

Taylor didn't tell her moms what was happening.

school who knew she had two moms didn't seem to care. But it was different in middle school. Just getting through the day without breaking down in tears was a challenge.

Talk About It

- **What do you think it would be like to have two moms? What would be good? What would be bad?**

- **Why do you think Taylor didn't tell her moms what was happening at school?**

Then one day, Taylor was eating lunch by herself when a boy named Alex asked if he could sit with her. Alex was cute, and a lot of girls had crushes on him. At first, they talked about how bad the food was. Then Alex asked her if she could keep a secret.

"The thing is," said Alex in a low voice, "I live with my dad . . . and my other dad. But you can't tell anyone because . . . well, you know."

Alex went on to tell her how he'd been teased, bullied, and even beaten up at his last school. It had gotten so bad that his family had moved so he could go to a new school. Now he was careful to make sure no one found out. Taylor thought about what it would be like to have to hide her parents from people. Then she thought about the big risk Alex had taken by trusting her with his secret.

"Why did you tell me?" she asked.

"I don't know. I have a lot of friends at this school, but I doubt they'd still be my friends if they knew about my dads. I figured that it wouldn't matter to you. And also . . . I've kind of liked you since the beginning of the year."

Taylor and Alex started hanging out together every day. Taylor felt relieved to finally be able to talk to someone who understood.

Talk About It

- **What do you think would happen if Alex's friends found out about his two dads?**

- **Has anyone ever trusted you with a really big secret? How did that feel?**

- **Have you ever had a friend who you felt really understood you? What kinds of things did you talk about?**

Ask Dr. Robyn

Sometimes children raised by same-sex parents are treated differently than other children. Some people are homophobic or have religious beliefs that are not favorable toward gays and lesbians. They may treat gays and lesbians—as well as the children who are raised by them—unfairly and disrespectfully. A girl who is raised in a same-sex family may choose to hide that fact because she is afraid of being teased or bullied. However, this is a difficult thing to hide. Most likely, the truth will come out.

A girl raised in a same-sex family may decide to hide her own sexuality. If she is straight, she might feel that her parents will be disappointed that she is not a lesbian. If she has feelings for other girls, she may hide them because she doesn't want other people to think that she became a lesbian because she was raised by gay or lesbian parents. It really doesn't matter if your parents are gay or straight. What really matters is that they love and accept you for who you are.

Get Healthy

1. No matter what your sexual orientation is, there is no need to feel ashamed of it. You don't need to prove that you are straight or lesbian. You just need to be yourself.

2. You don't have to tell your peers that you come from a same-sex household. However, it might be a good idea to tell a few of your closest and most trusted friends. It is good to have friends you can talk to openly.

3. There are many studies that show children raised by gay and lesbian parents are just as healthy and happy as those raised by heterosexual parents. If there is someone in your life who is having a hard time accepting your family situation, it might help to educate him or her.

4. Try not to let intolerant people get to you. Remember that most people who bully others are just trying to bolster their own low self-images.

The Last Word from Rachel

Having same-sex parents can make you feel caught in the middle. No matter what your sexual orientation, people may make assumptions about you based on your parents. It can be easy to be angry with your parents for not being part of a traditional family. Remember that your parents care for you deeply. They are there to support you when things get difficult. After all, it's the love that makes the family!

10

The New Mom

Fairy tales such as Cinderella and Snow White have given stepmothers a bad reputation. Although most real stepmothers are not actually evil, they can be a source of hurt feelings and frustration for a girl who is trying to adjust to a new stepfamily. A girl may feel like she has to compete with her stepmother for her father's attention. The stepmother may expect her new stepdaughter to follow new rules and to do things differently than she has before. This can be especially challenging during adolescence when a girl is becoming more independent. She may not welcome another person's rules or opinions. Lucy was happy that her father was getting remarried, but she didn't know that things would change so much when his girlfriend became her stepmother.

Lucy's Story

Lucy's parents divorced when she was eight years old. They shared custody, so Lucy lived for a week with her father and then a week with her mother. Lucy's mom stayed single, but her father had recently remarried. Lucy was happy when her father told her that he and Anna were getting married.

Lucy's mom stayed single, but her father had recently remarried.

She liked Anna and was excited about the wedding. More importantly, she wanted her father to be happy, and Anna seemed to make him happy. But when Anna moved in, things began to change.

When Lucy's dad and Anna had been dating, Anna never tried to tell Lucy what to do. She'd been friendly and easygoing. Now she suddenly seemed to be taking over everything. First it was the house. When Lucy's dad had moved out of her mom's house, he'd taken some of the older furniture to furnish his new place. The best thing in his house was the big blue couch. It had come from their old family room. It wasn't in the best shape, but it was really comfortable, and it had been in the family since before Lucy was born. A few weeks after the wedding, Lucy had arrived for her week with Dad to find that Anna had redecorated the entire living room. The big blue couch was gone, and in its place there was a fancy white sofa. Lucy hated the new sofa. It was hard and uncomfortable, and Anna wouldn't let them put their feet on it, even if they weren't wearing shoes. Lucy felt as if she weren't at home in her own living room.

Talk About It

- **What do you think it would be like to live a week at one parent's house and then a week at the other parent's house?**

- **Have your parents divorced and remarried others? If so, how did it feel? If not, how do you think it would feel?**

- **Why do you think Anna changed after she moved in with Lucy's dad?**

Then Anna started telling Lucy what to do. It had started at dinner. According to Anna, Lucy had terrible table manners. Anna said things such as "elbows off the table" and "don't slurp your soup." Everything Lucy did seemed to be wrong.

One day, Lucy was about to go to a friend's house when Anna stopped her. "You aren't going out like that, are you?" Anna asked.

Lucy looked at her outfit. She was wearing torn jeans and a T-shirt. "Like what?" she asked.

"You look like a bum in those torn jeans."

"I'm just going over to Kaitlyn's. Honestly, no one cares. Besides, these are my favorite jeans."

"Well, I don't think it's appropriate for a girl your age to dress that way. What will Kaitlyn's mother think?" said Anna. "Go change into something else."

"I'm not going to change." Lucy could feel her voice rising. "You can't tell me what to do. You aren't my mother. I'll wear these jeans if I want!" Lucy stormed out the door, slamming it behind her.

She didn't look back, but she heard Anna shouting after her. "You get back here, young lady. Don't you walk away when I am talking to you!"

Lucy kept walking, but she had to turn around as soon as she got to Kaitlyn's. Anna had called Kaitlyn's mom and told her Lucy did not have permission to go out. Kaitlyn's mom sent her back home. Lucy couldn't believe it. She and Kaitlyn were supposed to work on a school project. Anna had no right to do this! Anna said something about wanting to talk to Lucy when she walked in, but Lucy ignored her and went straight to her room.

Lucy kept walking, but she had to turn around as soon as she got to Kaitlyn's.

Talk About It

- Do you think Anna had a right to tell Lucy to change her jeans? Why or why not?

- Do you think Anna handled the situation well? What about Lucy? What could each have done differently?

- Have you ever had to be around someone who criticized you a lot? What did it feel like?

Later, Lucy's dad knocked on her door.

"Anna is very upset about the way you treated her today," he said.

Lucy looked at him in disbelief. "The way I treated her? What about the way she treated me?"

"I know Anna can be a little . . . demanding sometimes. But you need to remember that she has never had kids of her own. She doesn't always know how to treat a teenage girl."

"That's for sure," said Lucy glumly. "I just wish she'd stop telling me what to do all the time."

"Well, I certainly don't want my two favorite girls fighting. How about coming downstairs and we can all discuss it over ice cream?"

Lucy thought about it. She wasn't sure if she was ready to face Anna just yet. After a minute, she nodded. Maybe a good talk would start to set things right.

Talk About It

- **What do you think it would be like to suddenly be the stepmother of a teenage girl, especially if you had never had children of your own?**

- **Do you think Lucy should try to work things out with Anna? What could Lucy say to Anna to help this situation?**

- **What do you think of the way Lucy's dad wanted to address things?**

Ask Dr. Robyn

Adjusting to a new stepparent is not always easy. A girl may see a new stepparent as an unwelcome intruder who will change the way things are done in her family. Most families have an established set of rules, routines, and ways of doing things. A new stepparent may have different expectations. This can be frustrating for a girl, especially if the stepparent's new rules are stricter than the old ones.

Like Lucy, a girl might lose her temper when her stepmother tries to tell her what to do. If the parent supports his or her new spouse, the stepdaughter may feel that her parent is taking the new stepparent's side. This can really hurt her feelings and make her feel like she is alone in the family.

When a new stepparent moves in, a new family is instantly created; however, that does not mean that you actually feel like a family. Relationships take time. It takes time to feel comfortable around a new person. A girl may feel pressured to treat her new stepparent like her real parent. Talking about your feelings and taking things slowly can really help. If stepparents and stepchildren communicate and respect each other's feelings, things will go more smoothly.

Get Healthy

1. Try to communicate your feelings to your parent and your stepparent. If it's too hard to tell them how you feel, try writing your feelings in a note.

2. Pick your battles. Try to let go of the things that don't really matter much. If your stepparent thinks of you as cooperative, he or she is more likely to give in when something is really important to you.

3. Try to treat your new stepparent politely and with respect. Kindness can go a long way. You don't have to love someone to treat that person kindly.

4. Give your stepparent a chance. It's easy to focus on the negative. However, if you get to know each other, you may have more in common than you think.

The Last Word from Rachel

Even though stepfamilies can be challenging, they can also be rewarding. As you get to know and trust your new stepparent more, you may start to get along better too. If your stepparent understands your feelings, he or she may be able to change the way that he or she treats you so that everyone gets what they need. Someday you may find yourself going to your stepparent for advice and support.

A Second Look

As an adolescent girl, you are learning more about who you are and who you want to be in the world. Your family is a big part of that. They likely influence your opinions, values, and, perhaps most importantly, your self-esteem.

All of the girls in this book came from non-traditional families, and although they all faced challenges, each one of them can still grow into a strong, confident, happy adult. They may each feel different from their peers and may wish they had been born into "normal" families. But the truth is, no one really knows what "normal" is. Even families that seem to fit the traditional mold, with both parents and their kids living in the same house, might very well have big challenges of their own.

Some of the girls in this book were fortunate enough to have supportive families. It can be challenging to have a sibling with special needs, to have a parent in the military, to be raised by same-sex parents, or to be adopted. But a girl who has a strong relationship with her parents will probably be able to talk to them about her feelings—and that can really help! Some of the other girls were not so fortunate. If a girl is a foster child, or if she has a parent who is addicted to drugs or alcohol or is in prison, she may need to look outside her family for help and support.

I hope that as you explore your relationship with your own family, you learn positive ways to cope with difficult situations. It is important to remember that you control your own behavior and if things are not going well, you can always make a different choice.

XOXO,
Rachel

Pay It Forward

Remember, a healthful life is about balance. Now that you know how to walk that path, pay it forward to a friend or even to yourself! Remember the Get Healthy tips throughout this book, and then take these steps to get healthy and get going.

- Talking about your feelings can really help! If you are struggling with a parent, try talking to him or her. If you can't talk to your parent, find another adult you can trust who can help you work out your feelings.

- Remember that it's okay to have negative feelings. You might feel angry, resentful, sad, embarrassed, or frustrated. However, it's important that you express your feelings in healthy ways, such as writing them down in a journal or talking with someone you trust.

- Everyone needs a break sometimes. It's okay to spend time with friends, join an after-school activity, or even spend time away with relatives or at summer camp. It's also okay to take quiet time for yourself.

- If you are taking on too many adult responsibilities, talk to your parents to see if they can find ways to lighten the load. Remember, you are still a kid, so it's important that you take the time to be one.

- If your family is facing serious problems and you don't feel safe at home, you need to tell a trustworthy adult outside your home. If your parent is not protecting you, you need to protect yourself.

- Find peers who share some of your challenges. Join a support group of other teens or find someone who has a family situation similar to yours. Even one friend can make a difference in your life.

- Treating people kindly and politely can go a long way. You can always choose to conduct yourself in a way that makes you feel good about your own behavior.

- Don't give in to the victim mentality. You may be dealing with some hard situations, but wallowing in negative thoughts won't help. Look for the good things in your life and try to keep a positive attitude.

- Try not to take the comments of intolerant people personally. People who are unkind to others who are different from themselves are usually insecure.

- Remember that your parents are doing the best they can. Even if they have made poor choices, in most cases they still want what is best for you. If your parents have done very hurtful things, it can be hard to forgive them, but forgiving them will help you feel better and move forward.

Additional Resources

Select Bibliography

Eldridge, Sherry. *Twenty Things Adopted Kids Wish Their Adoptive Parents Knew.* New York: Dell Publishing, 1999.

Fuyo Gaskins, Pearl. *What Are You? Voices of Mixed-Race Young People.* New York: Henry Holt, 1999.

Nelson, Aurealia N. *Non Traditional Families: The Impact on Our Children.* Lincoln, NE: Writers Club Press, 2001.

Toledo, Sylvie, and Deborah Elder Brown. *Grandparents as Parents—A Survival Guide for Raising a Second Family.* New York: Guilford Press, 1995.

Further Reading

Block, Joel D., and Susan Bartell. *Stepliving for Teens: Getting Along with Stepparents, Parents, and Siblings.* New York: Price Stern Sloan, 2001.

Gorbett, Danea. *Adopted Teens Only: A Survival Guide to Adolescence.* Lincoln, NE: Universe Star, 2007.

Lynch, Amy, et al. *Real Families: Figuring Out Your Family and Where You Fit In.* Middleton, WI: American Girl, 2007.

Meyer, Don, and David Gallagher. *The Sibling Slam Book: What It's Really Like to Have a Brother or Sister with Special Needs.* Bethesda, MD: Woodbine House, 2005.

Web Sites

To learn more about nontraditional families, visit ABDO Publishing Company online at **www.abdopublishing.com**. Web sites about nontraditional families are featured on our Book Links page. These links are routinely monitored and updated to provide the most current information available.

For More Information

For more information on this subject, contact or visit the following organizations.

Alateen

1600 Corporate Landing Parkway
Virginia Beach, VA 23454-5617
757-563-1600
www.al-anon.alateen.org
Alateen supports teens who are living with alcoholics. Alateen groups meet in local communities throughout the United States and Canada.

Foster Club

753 First Avenue, Seaside, OR 97138
503-717-1552
www.fosterclub.com
This organization sponsors a Web site with information for teens in foster care. There are articles, message boards, contests, and more.

Glossary

abusive
Treating a person cruelly and inhumanely.

addiction
Being physically or psychologically dependent on something.

alcoholic
A person who is addicted to alcohol.

autism
A developmental disorder involving impaired speech, poor social skills, repetitive behaviors, and limited interests.

convicted
To be found guilty of a crime in a court of law.

deploy
To move soldiers to where they are needed.

gay
A person who is sexually attracted to people of the same sex.

group home
A small, supervised facility where children who do not have homes may live for a period of time.

heterosexual
A person who is sexually attracted to people of the opposite sex.

homophobic
 Having an irrational hatred of gay and lesbian people.

incarcerated
 To be put in prison.

intoxicated
 Drunk.

lesbian
 A woman who is sexually attracted to other women.

neglect
 To not care for someone properly.

self-esteem
 Confidence in oneself.

sexual orientation
 The direction of a person's sexual interest toward the opposite sex, the same sex, or both.

tolerance
 The ability to accept people who are different or who have different views than oneself.

Index

About the Author

Rachel Lynette has written more than 40 books
for children and teens. She is also the author of
several teacher resource books. She holds a degree in
developmental psychology and has a background in
highly capable education. Rachel lives in the Seattle area
with her two teenage children, David and Lucy, and a cat
named Cosette. When she isn't writing or researching,
Rachel enjoys spending time with her family and friends,
traveling, reading, drawing, biking, and in-line skating.

Photo Credits